Jody the mouse, is a magical toy. He was fashioned by The Wizard of Paint Creek. The Wizard is a skilled toy maker, who endows his toys with magical qualities - qualities only apparent to children with imagination.

Jody understands and speaks every language there is. He, and all the other mice that the Wizard made, know many wonderful things, which they share with those who believe in them.

Katie Murphy believed in Jody from the start. He became her family's guide on their trips through Michigan.

Jody's Michigan Adventure Books tell about all the things that happened to Jody, and Katie's other animal friends. You are invited to come along with the Murphy family. All you need to do is enter into Katie's imagination . . .

Great Places
Jody's Michigan Adventures
Michigan's Holland

Summary: The Murphy family visits
Holland, Michigan. Kevin Murphy and his little
sister Katie argue about where to eat. Left alone on
the lawn of the Historic Pillar Church, Katie's toy
mouse, Jody, meets Flower the skunk. The two
animals compare their impressions of the city. Jody
tells Katie his version of what he saw. She insists
that her brother Kevin include the mouse's
story in his computer travelogue.

Written by Leigh A. Arrathoon & John J. Davio
Illustrated by Jeanne L. Morris & Kenneth M. Hajdyla
Coloring by Mary Anne Strong

If you want more information on
Great Places, write for a free brochure
Paint Creek Press, Ltd.
P.O. Box 80547, Rochester, MI 48308-0001

ISBN 1-893047-03-2

Printed in China

Katie Murphy

Kevin Murphy

Mike Murphy

Mary Murphy

Jody

Flower

I remember that it was a warm May afternoon. My little sister, Katie Murphy, had set Jody, her toy Dutch mouse, down on the grass near the Historic Pillar Church in Holland, Michigan. In case you were wondering, my name is Kevin Murphy.

Katie and I were arguing about what to eat. Katie wanted pizza. The rest of the family wanted to go to the Queen's Inn for some real Dutch food.

"Look," I said. "It says here that the Queen's Inn has a windmill. Part of its roof is **thatched** (made of straw). Inside, it has a wooden beam ceiling and an open hearth fireplace."

"So?" This is Katie's favorite answer. She learned it from me.

"Katie," I said patiently. "How many times do we get to do something cool like this?"

Since Katie and I were arguing, Jody, the toy mouse, watched the people leaving the afternoon parade. Floats were making their way back down the street. There were also **Klompen dancers** (people dressed in Dutch costumes, who danced in their wooden shoes).

A red wagon was being pulled by six little horses. None of these animals was any taller than a child. They were those perfect miniature horses that have been in the world since the **Pleistocene era**. (A time about 70,000,000 years ago!)

There was also a spirited black horse. It was a stallion. It broke away from its master, who had to chase it down the street. Everyone ran after the man to see if he could catch the horse.

Jody was sitting on the grass under a shade tree. He told Katie later that it was lovely there. A large creature came creeping towards him. It had white fur on its head and back. The rest of it was black. Jody thought he ought to speak to it.

Jody told Katie that Flower really wasn't so bad, once you got to know her. Flower told him that she and her family made a yearly journey along Shore Line Drive, in Holland, to Macatawa State Park. They would see huge, elegant houses and big boats. At length, they would come to a place where they could cross over onto the sand.

The beach was filled with cottages. The surrounding hills were dotted with charming, old homes. At the other side of the beach, was the bright red Macatawa Holland Harbor Lighthouse. It looks out over the shoreline of Lake Michigan.

"The wind always blows there. The sun is warm on our faces. The sand feels cold on my feet, as I thrust them beneath it. You can see up and down the beach and far out onto the lake," Flower sighed.

Flower began thinking about the lighthouse. It stood in the middle of a **shoal** (a narrow, shallow piece of land that sticks out into the water). Her family liked to climb up the tower to get a view of the lake.

"Humans have to get permission to do this, because the lighthouse is private property," she said. "But we skunks just go where we please."

"That's nice," Jody said. "I have to go where I'm taken, and I'm not always thrilled."

"What do you mean?" asked Flower.

"Well, take this visit to Holland," Jody said. "I've loved most of it, but it hasn't all been wonderful."

As he spoke, he began to remember the events of the last two days. "It all began at a craft show," he explained.

"A craft show?" Flower looked puzzled.

"Yes, my master, the Wizard of Paint Creek, is a skilled toymaker. He made many of us mice. After he had fashioned us, he enchanted us, endowing us with magical qualities. He sells us at craft shows all over the world."

"Magical?" said Flower. "How?"

"For one thing, we talk. Not only do I speak 'skunk,' but I can also speak every language there is! And I know many things."

"Oh," said Flower. She wasn't sure what to say to this magical mouse.

"Anyway, the Murphy family came to the craft show," Jody continued. "The little girl, Katie, is a clever child. She began to talk to me. When I answered her, she wasn't the least bit surprised.

I told her I was Jody, the Dutch mouse. If she bought me, I would be her guide. I could show her around the *Tulpen Feest* (Dutch Festival).

Katie loved me instantly. She begged her father to buy me. He always buys stuffed animals for her, wherever the family goes. Katie told him I was special, but he didn't pay much attention to her. Then she announced to anyone who would listen:

We're going to the Tulpen Feest. Jody, the magical Dutch mouse is going to be our guide!

"And that's how it all began.

When we got to Holland, I gave Katie directions to *DeZwann*, which means 'The Swan.' You probably know it's the oldest Dutch windmill in America. It's over 200 years old. They still make flour there!"

The skunk didn't seem to know about the windmill, but she nodded politely.

"Katie was excited," Jody continued. "She bounced up and down and made me dance.

I told her that DeZwann was part of Windmill Island. They have 100,000 tulips. I could hardly wait to scamper through them.

My Uncle Hans told me about the **draalmolen** (merry-go-round) they have there too. I wanted to ride on it, and so did Katie. Katie's father was a little skeptical. I don't think he believed I knew where I was going."

"Mrs. Murphy loved the tulips. Later she wanted to see all the tulip lanes that line the streets in downtown Holland!

After a while, five-year-old Katie had had her fill of the children's zoo on Windmill Island. She also tired of racing around DeZwann.

I got sick of being dragged upside-down through the tulips. I suggested we go to Dutch Village. It looks like the Holland in Europe. The houses have **stepped gables** (the pointed ends of the houses look like stairs or steps). I knew the village is north on US 31. Mr. Murphy drove us there. He kept saying, *How does Jody know all this Katie?*"

"Dutch Village is a fabulous place, but it turned into a disaster for me.

The village has brick streets that run along canals. There are pretty bridges across the water. One we went over was arched. It was made of brick. The road part was **planked** (made out of wood).

We walked along the sea wall, munchng on the Dutch candy we had bought at one of the shops.

Then wc found a place with a witches' scale - **Hexenwaag** in Dutch. This scale was made in 1708. Mr. Murphy talked his wife into getting weighed. Mrs. Murphy wasn't crazy about this idea. A small crowd had already gathered to watch her.

Mr. Murphy likes his wife because she's a good sport. I can't say the same for him. He said he was too heavy. If he got on the scale, he was sure he would break it."

"We finally found a bench next to the canal. We stopped there to eat some Dutch cheese and bread we had bought. We also had some cookies. I was really getting into the cheese, when Katie dragged me off by the arm and threw me into the water.

Hey! What did you do that for? I screamed.

Oh, oh. Katie said, as she crouched down on the side of the seawall. The next thing I knew, she was thrashing around in the water, crying for help.

Mrs. Murphy jumped into the canal. She was still wearing her blue jeans. She caught hold of one of Katie's skinny arms and pulled her back to the side of the canal. Mr. Murphy lifted Katie onto shore. Kevin helped his mother back onto the sea wall. In the excitement, no one thought about me, floating quietly downstream."

"Katie was coughing and crying. Kevin, of course, felt helpless and angry. He was afraid his little sister might die. How could she drown in less than four feet of water?! He never gave me a single thought.

Mr. and Mrs. Murphy were worried about Katie. Mr. Murphy bent over the child, rubbing her between the shoulder blades to make her spit up any water she might have swallowed. I tried to wave, but no one noticed me."

"Katie did stop coughing. But then she started to wail. A man stepped out of the crowd.

I'm a doctor! said the stranger. He leaned over Katie and examined her.

Jody is drowning! Katie sputtered. *He fell in the canal. I tried to get him. Please save Jody!*

Well, at least somebody was thinking about me! Not Mr. Murphy. *We'll buy a new Jody*, he growled.

Luckily for me a kind old man fished me out with his cane."

"The doctor showed us to a nearby hotel where Katie and I could dry out. We stayed over night. The big parade was the next day.

When we were sure that Katie was okay, we went back into the Dutch Village to do some more sightseeing. A lot of the houses there were brick, with clay tile roofs - just like in the old country. They also had an old time wedding wagon and a mail wagon.

The Klompen dancers came out to perform to the music of the Amsterdam Street Organ.

Every fifteen minutes craftsmen showed how they made fudge, hand-carved shoes, or candles. Mrs. Murphy, Katie, and I watched the candlemakers. Mr. Murphy and Kevin went on the **Zweefmolen** (a neat swinging chair carousel). They said that was very exciting."

"Kevin wants to become an historian. His mother always takes him to museums. In Holland, they visited the Herrick Public Library and the Holland Museum so Kevin could learn how the Dutch settlers lived. They also visited the Cappon House, built in 1873-74. Isaac Cappon was Dutch. He was penniless when he arrived in Holland, Michigan. But he later became the city's first mayor.

Engbertus van der Veen was Kevin's favorite character. He wrote **memoirs** (a personal account of hard times).

Engbertus was one of the first people to settle in Michigan. He left Amsterdam with his father in 1847. He wrote that when his family arrived in Holland, Michigan they were very upset because it was a wild, scary place.

It was 'really a dense forest of big trees . . . the air was full of malaria caused by the swamp, stagnant water, and dirty waters of Black Lake - a place of sickness and death.' ''*

*From *The Making of Michigan, 1820-1860*: a Pioneer Anthology. Ed. Justin L. Kestenbaum (Wayne State University Press, 1990), pp. 181-206.

"Engbertus' mother wanted to go back to Amsterdam right away. The family camped for two months. They hoped a ship would come to take them home. Finally they realized they had to stay in the terrifying wilderness.

Life in America must have been rough at first, but the Dutch were hard workers and very brave. In the Netherlands, there weren't many trees, so the people built their homes with brick. In America they had to build wooden houses and roads. This meant they had to learn to chop down trees for lumber.

At first the Hollanders would chop all around the tree trunks. They didn't know that a tree standing in the middle of a stump could fall in any direction. Trees sometimes fell on people's houses and crushed them.

The only roads were the Indian trails. The Dutch made 'log bridges' across the low wet spots in these trails. Engbertus didn't like the log roads much because he says,

Riding over such a bridge in a lumber wagon drawn by oxen was a severe trial. The shaking made me sick in my stomach."

"The family built a fire. *The moaning sounds of the western pine, the night birds squawking and shrilly breaking into weird cries, the hooting of owls, and the croaking of a multitude of strange creatures . . .* frightened them."

"The new settlers didn't understand Indian ways. When the Hollanders saw **venison** (deer meat) hanging from trees, they thought nobody wanted it. They took the meat down and ate it. This made the Indians mad. They had hung that meat out to cure, so it would taste better.

The Indians used to plant corn and beans before they went north to hunt. The Hollanders found the rich fields the Indians had left behind. They figured the Indians didn't want this land anymore. They took the corn and bean fields and divided them amongst themselves.

Then the Indians returned from the hunt. They must have been looking forward to some tasty corn on the cob. Imagine how annoyed they were when they saw their new neighbors harvesting their food. I guess the Indians lost patience with the Dutch. They sold them all their land. Then they moved away."

"In between visits to the museum, we got to watch Klompen dancers. Katie and Kevin wanted wooden shoes, but Mr. Murphy was afraid the children would fall or kick someone.

This afternoon, the mayor and city council inspected the streets. They said that 8th Street was dirty.

Dutch men came out with pails of water. The pails were hung from wooden yokes across the men's shoulders. Dutch women scrubbed the pavements with brushes and brooms.

After the street scrubbing, there was a colorful Volksparade. Everyone dressed the way the early settlers did back in the 1800s.

See how much I've learned in just two days Flower?" Jody said.

The skunk wasn't listening. "See ya!" she grinned. With that she pounced on a little field mouse, who had wandered across the lawn.

Well, that was the part of the story Jody told to Katie. I guess it's up to me to tell the rest as I saw it.

"Jody! Jody! I was looking all over for you! Come on!" my sister called. "It's all settled. I get pizza. Then we're going to the Queen's Inn."

With that, she snatched Jody up by the bad arm and dragged him off to the Pizza shop.

After the Tulip Festival was over, my parents decided to drive south on U.S. 31 a few miles to Saugatuck. That town is a colorful artist's colony on Lake Kalamazoo. Flower had disappeared, so Jody had nothing better to do.

We got into Saugatuck as the sun was setting. The water was black, but the sky was a bright navy blue. You could still see red and gold reflections from the sun shimmering on the water's surface.

That night we had our dinner at The Mermaids. It was in the Dockside Marketplace, overlooking the water. We had a hard time deciding between this place and Coral Gables, another restaurant with a view of the water. I guess both of them have fireplaces. My mother wished she could come back in the winter so she could eat by the fire. I wished we could go on the Star of Saugatuck, a paddleboat ride.

There were over thirty bed and breakfasts in Saugatuck. We finally chose one.

Katie woke up screaming in the middle of the night. "Mommy, Mommy!" she sobbed. "I dreamt I couldn't breathe."

"Well that's what happens when you jump into the canal after a stuffed mouse, and you don't know how to swim. Maybe next time you'll ask me or daddy to help you," said my mom.

"Maybe I'll take swimming lessons," Katie suggested.

"Well that's okay with me. But, for now, if Jody falls into any more water - even a puddle, you let me or daddy get him for you, okay?"

"Okay, Mommy," Katie replied with a yawn, as she drifted back to sleep.

The next morning, after breakfast, we went out to explore the town. Katie wanted to pat the fat ducks and geese waddling along the street.

When we got home, Katie chattered to Jody in Hollmouse and Klompen danced with him for hours. He told her what happened to him while the family was in Holland. Katie told me everything Jody said. She made sure I typed his part of the story on the computer as well as mine.

Jody joined the family every morning at breakfast after that. Katie fed him jam. Soon his fur was sticky. I read him the comics.

"If he doesn't understand English, why am I reading to him?" I asked.

"Jody speaks perfect English. He just doesn't feel like it," my sister snapped. "In fact, Jody speaks every language there is." And that is how Jody came to be the official family "interpreter."